THE WELL WOMAN
A 15 Day Devotional
FOR WOMEN THAT NEED TO KNOW **WHO** LOVE IS

Joy Mullins

JP

Name: Joy Mullins
Title: "The Well Woman: A 15 Day Devotional
For Women That Need To Know Who Love Is."
Cite/References
(2002-2004). What do the different names of God mean?
https://www.gotquestions.org/names-of-God.html (2024).
Names of God. https://www.lwf.org
The Holy Bible, New International Version. (2011). Bible
Gateway. https://www.biblegateway.com/versions/New

ISBN: (Paperback)

Front cover image & Book designed by Joyner Publishing.
Printed in the United States of America.
First printing edition 2023

JP | Joyner Publishing
Tampa, FL, 33547
www.joynerpublishing.com
services@joynerpublishing.com

Contents

Dedication

I would like to dedicate this devotional to my sisters who are
struggling to find their way in the dark.
And to Patricia, thank you for all your wisdom and
guidance.

GOD SEES YOU

JOHN 4 NIV

Now Jesus learned that the Pharisees had heard that he was gaining and baptizing more disciples than John— 2 although in fact it was not Jesus who baptized, but his disciples. 3 So he left Judea and went back once more to Galilee. 4 Now he had to go through Samaria. 5 So he came to a town in Samaria called Sychar, near the plot of ground Jacob had given to his son Joseph. 6 Jacob's well was there, and Jesus, tired as he was from the journey, sat down by the well. It was about noon. 7 When a Samaritan woman came to draw water, Jesus said to her, "Will you give me a drink?" 8 (His disciples had gone into the town to buy food.) 9 The Samaritan woman said to him, "You are a Jew and I am a Samaritan woman. How can you ask me for a drink?" (For Jews do not associate with Samaritans. 10 Jesus answered her, "If you knew the gift of God and who it is that asks you for a drink, you would have asked him and he would have given you living water." 11 "Sir," the woman said, "you have nothing to draw with and the well is deep. Where can you get this living water? 12 Are you greater than our father Jacob, who gave us the well and drank from it himself, as did also his sons and his livestock?" 13 Jesus answered, "Everyone who drinks this water will be thirsty again, 14 but whoever drinks the water I give them will never thirst. Indeed, the water I give them will become in them a spring of water welling up to eternal life." 15 The woman said to him, "Sir, give me this water so that I won't get thirsty and have to keep coming here to draw water." 16 He told her, "Go, call your husband and come back." 17 "I have no husband," she replied. Jesus said to her, "You are right when you say you have no husband. 18 The fact is, you have had five husbands, and the man you now have is not your husband. What you have just said is quite true." 19 "Sir," the woman said, "I can see that you are a prophet.

20 Our ancestors worshiped on this mountain, but you Jews claim that the place where we must worship is in Jerusalem."21 "Woman," Jesus replied, "believe me, a time is coming when you will worship the Father neither on this mountain nor in Jerusalem. 22 You Samaritans worship what you do not know; we worship what we do know, for salvation is from the Jews. 23 Yet a time is coming and has now come when the true worshipers will worship the Father in the Spirit and in truth, for they are the kind of worshipers the Father seeks. 24 God is spirit, and his worshipers must worship in the Spirit and in truth." 25 The woman said, "I know that Messiah" (called Christ) "is coming. When he comes, he will explain every-thing to us." 26 Then Jesus declared, "I, the one speaking to you—I am he."

I always loved this passage of scripture, it's one of my favorites. It truly resonates with me. Jesus sent His disciples to get food before He talked to the woman at the well. I can imagine how embarrassed and shameful the woman would have felt if Jesus had discussed her business (being married not once, two, or three times, but five! And currently living with a man who is not her husband) in front of His disciples. Yet, Jesus did NOT do this. He meets with her alone, one on-one, and intentionally does not humiliate her in front of other men. ***He went out His way to talk to her and already knew about her situation and her past.*** How awesome is that? God loves us, women, so much that He gives thought to how we feel and what we are going through. Not only that, but He also protects us from shame. I'm not only in awe of what Jesus did or said, but what He did NOT do or say. He did not dismiss this woman who was divorced five times, He was not disgusted with her, in fact she was the first person revealed Himself to as the Messiah. ***She did not leave His presence feeling ashamed, but she was changed and free!***

Note to Self ...

Day 1

What do you expect?

Have you ever expected someone to love you the way you loved them, but they did not? Have you ever expected someone to treat you the same way you treated them, only to be subject to injury? Let me explain this from a relational standpoint. You cannot change anyone, yes, even a man, no matter what you do for them or how hard you try. It's not your job. Stop expecting someone to make you happy or feel complete. Stop expecting someone to live up to your standards when they simply can't. ***When you do this, you're dehumanizing the person involved by making them a mere object to satisfy your needs or fill up space where there is lack.*** There is nothing wrong with expecting the best out of someone you love, but it is wrong to expect them to give you what they cannot give. This long and painful journey of giving only to receive nothing in return leads to devastation. You create an idol in your life that replaces God. ***An idol that can't love you back.***

Expect God to love you unconditionally because He does. Expect God to fill that emptiness, that void in your heart, because He will.

PSALM 62: 5

My soul wait silently for God alone,
For my expectation is from Him.

El Elyon

El Elyon is one of the names of God used in the Old Testament. It means God most high or Lord most high. This name refers to the LORD, the creator of heaven and earth. Since God is the highest or most high this means there is no idol, god, or creature that should be worshiped or exalted over the Lord because He is superior to all things, in every way.

References
(Psalm 57:2, Deuteronomy 26:19)

Reflection

Do you know how much God loves you? Do you know that
God loves you…period? No strings attached, unconditionally.
Ask God to show you His love for you today.

_____

_____

_____

_____

_____

_____

_____

_____

_____

_____

_____

_____

_____

_____

_____

_____

_____

_____

_____

_____

Day 2

Just Breathe Girl!

Life's troubles and difficulties can often feel like a heavy weight settling right in the middle of your chest. Life can even seem unbearable and overwhelming. The weight of your circumstances and experiences does not feel like it's diminishing, no matter what you do. You begin to drown. ***Every breath you take is a desperate attempt to simply survive the day or even the moment.***

Take a minute to pause, digress, and breathe. Tell God about your worries, struggles, fears, anger, and anxious thoughts. He already knows them. Say it to Him audibly to get the weight off you. He will restore you if you let go and give it to Him. He sees and cares for you. You were not created to figure out everything on your own. Give thanks to God for that!

I'm writing to YOU, the single mom, the "Ms. Independent," ***the woman whose default solution to every problem is herself.*** Pause, give thanks to God, let it go, and breathe! I know you're thinking, "***easier said than done***"...you are correct! It's so much easier said than done but start somewhere.

MATTHEW 6: 27-34

27 Can any one of you by worrying add a single hour to your life? 28 "And why do you worry about clothes? See how the flowers of the field grow. They do not labor or spin. 29 Yet I tell you that not even Solomon in all his splendor was dressed like one of these. 30 If that is how God clothes the grass of the field, which is here today and tomorrow is thrown into the fire, will he not much more clothe you—you of little faith? 31 So do not worry, saying, 'What shall we eat?' or 'What shall we drink?' or 'What shall we wear?' 32 For the pagans run after all these things, and your heavenly Father knows that you need them. 33 But seek first his kingdom and his righteousness, and all these things will be given to you as well. 34 Therefore do not worry about tomorrow, for tomorrow will worry about itself. Each day has enough trouble of its own.

El-Roi

El-Roi (The Hebrew name for God) "God who sees me."
"God of seeing." When you feel lonely and abandoned by
people you love or rely on, know that God is with you always.
He sees you, and He knows you by name. He hears the cry of
your heart, and He loves you more than you can ever imagine.

Reference
(Genesis 16:13)

Reflection

How long will you hold on to your pain? Are you ready to give it to God? Write down your thoughts or even a prayer. This is for YOU. What is on your mind right now?

_____

_____

_____

_____

_____

_____

_____

_____

_____

_____

_____

_____

_____

_____

_____

_____

_____

_____

_____

Day 3

True Self

On the journey to self-discovery, I was re-introduced to my true self. I can honestly say I was excited to meet her! Your true self is who you are, what you are, and Whose you are. Your true self is being, not doing.

For example, I currently work at a job that pays the bills. My occupation, however, is not who I am nor my sole purpose. My occupation does not define me. ***Aiming to be who God has called me to be through His Word and glorifying Him, wherever I am, is my purpose.*** I am far from perfect. I'm still growing and still have a lot of learning to do. ***This part of my life, my striving, and my growing, my imperfections and my failures, are still part of my purpose.***

Your purpose will speak to you in a whisper, and your true self will answer. Think back to when you were the most authentic version of yourself. You were most likely a child. What did you like, what did you dislike? Who did you admire? What types of people did you gravitate to? What were you naturally good at? What did you simply enjoy doing or not doing? God will show you who you were created to be. His purpose for your life has not changed because of your circumstances and the path you decided to take.

PSALM 139:1-6

1 You have searched me, Lord, and you know me. 2 You know when I sit and when I rise; you perceive my thoughts from afar. 3 You discern my going out and my lying down; you are familiar with all my ways. 4 Before a word is on my tongue you, Lord, know it completely. 5 You hem me in behind and before, and you lay your hand upon me. 6 Such knowledge is too wonderful for me, too lofty for me to attain.

El-Chuwl

El-Chuwl (Hebrew name for God), The God who gave you birth. God is our Creator and our Father. He saw us, and He loved us even before we were born. He has a plan for your life and if you walk with Him, He will fulfill His dreams over your life and amaze you.

Reference
(Psalm 139:13-18)

Reflection

Think about something you are passionate about. Are you stirring up your gift, or is it dormant?

_____

_____

_____

_____

_____

_____

_____

_____

_____

_____

_____

_____

_____

_____

_____

_____

_____

_____

_____

Day 4
What's Really Going On?

I love plants and have several in my home. Oftentimes, I am pretty good at determining their needs. Some plants like to be watered every other day, while some can go without water for an extended period of time. Some flourish in direct sunlight, while others can survive in the shade. If the leaves on the plant start to turn yellow, it's an indicator that I've possibly overwatered them. On the contrary, when the leaves turn brown, I probably have not watered them often enough.

However, there are a few occasions where I have no clue what is going on with them. Nothing I do seems to help them flourish. Sometimes, the plant will start to look unattractive or even dead. This is when I have to take it out of the pot and examine the roots. I then can determine if the plant has root rot, pests, or no roots at all! Whatever the case may be, it's usually a sign that something is terribly wrong. This is the same with you, with me, with all human life. Being depressed, angry, jealous, promiscuous, anorexic, or obese are just symptoms of rotten roots.

Some experiences took root in your life. Ask God what those experiences were (warning this may hurt a little). If you really   to change and heal, invite God in your life. You can simply start by praying and asking yourself why you behave the way you do or think the way you think. ***He will reveal it to you out of love, not condemnation.***

Most of the time, the problem is NOT the problem. The man you're with is not the problem, your parents are not the problem, your boss is not the problem. So, what's really going on? It's something much deeper. Remember, God wants to heal you from the inside out.

PSALM 51:10-12

10 Create in me a pure heart, O God, and renew a steadfast spirit within me. 11 Do not cast me from your presence or take your Holy Spirit from me. 12 Restore to me the joy of your salvation and grant me a willing spirit, to sustain me.

Jehovah-Rohi

Jehovah-Rohi (The Lord my shepherd) is one of the names of God used in one of the most familiar Psalms, Psalms 23. King David addresses the Lord as his shepherd. God cares for you, the way a shepherd tends and cares for his sheep. He leads you to still waters and green pastures.

Reference
(Psalm 23)

Reflection

Take a step to seek help and guidance from God. Pray for emotional, physical, spiritual, and mental healing. Decide to want to heal today.

_____

_____

_____

_____

_____

_____

_____

_____

_____

_____

_____

_____

_____

_____

_____

_____

_____

_____

_____

_____

_____

_____

Day 5
No More Selfies

We live in a time where everybody is concerned about themselves. Self-talk, self-love, self-care, self-discipline, and self-confidence are just a few ideologies. Not that these are bad attributes to have, but it's a little distorted. God said He created man in His image. I don't believe this truth is relevant to just how we look in the mirror. He created us in His image because we are His, and we are not to live our lives separate from Him. ***We can indulge in the concept of self-love, but how far is that really going to get anyone?***

It's temporary and somewhat of a delusion. Picture this. You have a beautiful baby girl. You have to love her, feed her, change her, and all the above to help her grow and thrive to get to the next stage of life. When she learns how to crawl, do you not think she needs your help to learn how to walk? Do you say, "I'm done. I've gotten you far enough?" Are you going to stop cooking her meals because she is able to feed herself with a spoon? Of course not! She can't live apart from you, and you, as a loving mom, know she can't and don't want her to. ***We are always going to be God's children; therefore, we will always need Him, and He wants us to know this.***

So, no more selfies. Replace self-confidence with confidence in the one Who created you. Don't strive for self-discipline, allow God to change you from the inside out.

John 15:5

"Yes, I am the vine; you are the branches. Those who remain in me, and I in them, will produce much fruit. For apart from me, you can do nothing."

Jehovah-M'Kaddesh

Jehovah-M'Kaddesh, the One who sanctifies, the One who makes us Holy as He is holy.

References
(Exodus 31:12-13; 1 Peter 1:15-16; Hebrews 13:12; 1 Thessalonians 5:23-24)

Reflection

You can do nothing apart from God. What "self" ideology are you embracing right now?

_____

_____

_____

_____

_____

_____

_____

_____

_____

_____

_____

_____

_____

_____

_____

_____

_____

_____

_____

_____

Day 6

Daddy Issues

"A dad is a son's first hero and a daughter's first love."
-Anonymous

What happens when your first love, Dad, abandons you, breaks your heart, abuses you, misguides you, or neglects you? *This pain, experience, and trauma sets the stage for scenes that will play out throughout your life.* Women will cling to the first man who shows them anything opposite of their reality. Even if the man is a counterfeit.

There is so much I can say on this topic, but I only want to focus on one point, that is, "that your earthly father and your Heavenly Father are two different beings." I know you know this, but *so many women (young and old) seem to hold a mirror up to their father and see God.* This is far from a fact. Your Heavenly Father loves you unconditionally. He will never abandon you. Do you know that *God does not enjoy seeing His daughters hurt and brokenhearted?* When you cry about what your earthly father has done to you or what pain he caused you, Jesus is right there with you.

In fact, Jesus says in *Mathew 11:28-30,* "Come to me, all you who are weary and burdened, and I will give you rest. Take my yoke upon you and learn from me, for I am gentle and humble in heart, and you will find rest for your souls. For my yoke is easy and my burden is light."

God promises in His word that He heals the brokenhearted and binds up their wounds, *Psalms 147:3.* What earthly father or anyone has said this to you and kept their word? ***Don't seek what your earthly father lacked to give you from someone else.*** It can't be done. God will be the only one that can fill you. God is your Father.

Abba

Abba is the Aramaic meaning for father. It's a term of affection, intimacy, and reverence for one's father. Jesus called God "Our Father" in Matthew 6:9, and He gave us that same privilege to call Him, Abba, or father as well.

References
(Mark 14:36; Romans 8:15)

Reflection

Meditate on these scriptures today.

"...So, you have not received a spirit that makes you fearful slaves. Instead, you received God's Spirit when he adopted you as his own children. Now we call him, "Abba, Father."

Romans 8:15

4 Sing to God, sing in praise of his name, extol him who rides on the clouds; rejoice before him—his name is the Lord. 5 A father to the fatherless, a defender of widows, is God in his holy dwelling.

Psalm 68:4-5

_____

_____

_____

_____

_____

_____

_____

_____

_____

_____

_____

_____

_____

_____

_____

_____

_____

Day 1

You Can't Fool You!

How many times have you said something to someone...or yourself but internally felt the opposite? For example, I have heard many women say, "I don't want to be in a relationship," yet they kept entertaining one. I'm guilty. I remember telling my friends, "I'm fine," but internally, I was feeling empty from agonizing loneliness. Or "I've moved on," but my mind and heart were stuck in heartbreak cement of heaviness, thwarting my ability to move forward.

You can't fool you! No one likes being lied to. We all know how it feels, yet you do it to yourself. **When the words you say don't line up with how you feel, it causes turmoil in your soul.** Say what you feel and how you feel to God. Be honest, be real, if not to yourself, to Him. Don't deceive yourself. **Verbalizing how you feel allows God to work and move miraculously in your life,** but most importantly, it deepens your relationship with Him.

PSALM 139:1-6

1 O Lord, you have searched me and known me! 2 You know when I sit down and when I rise up; you discern my thoughts from afar. 3 You search out my path and my lying down and are acquainted with all my ways. 4 Even before a word is on my tongue, behold, O Lord, you know it altogether. 5 You hem me in, behind and before, and lay your hand upon me. 6 Such knowledge is too wonderful for me; it is high; I cannot attain it.

Jehovah-Rapha

Jehovah-Rapha (The Lord who helps body and soul.)

Reference
(Exodus 15:26)

.

Reflection

What have you been lying to yourself about? Confess how you REALLY feel to God.

_____

_____

_____

_____

_____

_____

_____

_____

_____

_____

_____

_____

_____

_____

_____

_____

_____

_____

_____

_____

_____

Day 8
Is Jesus Enough?

I remember my experience at a healing conference a few years ago. It was life-changing! Near the end of the conference, one of the pastors asked us to sit still and allow the Holy Spirit to speak to us. I sat still. I was expecting God to say something like, "Work here, move here, or you're going to marry...." But, to my surprise, He asked me a thought-provoking question. ***"Is Jesus enough?"*** Of course, I thought to myself. However, reflecting on my life, my thoughts, actions, and words proved otherwise. I didn't realize how much I wanted Jesus to be the center of my life, but I also desired other things just as much. The people pleaser in me wanted to be liked by everyone I met. In the back of my mind, I really didn't know if I would be content if I was single for the next five years. I would even go far as to say I wasn't content with being where I was in my life, period.

I wanted to have certain friendships, a spouse, money, and a house. The list goes on and on. But I really had to reflect. ***If I didn't have the very thing my heart desired, would having Jesus in my life be enough?*** So, I'm going to ask you the same question the Holy Spirit asked me. "Is Jesus enough?" Do you desire more? Are you content with not having the things you desire right now? Be honest with yourself. I'm not implying that we don't need certain things in our lives, like friendships, money, etc. What I'm saying is that we have to trust that Jesus is all we need, and He will give us what we need. We are complete in Him. ***Don't go looking for anything outside of Him. Seek Him first.*** Allow Him to be the head, master, and ruler of your life.

PETER 1:3-4

3 His divine power has given us everything we need for a godly life through our knowledge of him, who called us by his own glory and goodness. 4 Through these he has given us his very great and precious promises, so that through them you may participate in the divine nature, having escaped the corruption in the world caused by evil desires.

Messiah, the anointed or Chosen one. The Gospels declare that Jesus is the Messiah or Christ—the One chosen by God and anointed by Him to save His people from their sins. He offers forgiveness of your sins and promises you salvation through Him.

References

(Matthew 16:16; Luke 4:17-21; John 1:40-49; 4:25, 26)

Reflection

Jesus is enough for you. Are there any relationships or "things" you desire more than Him?

_____

_____

_____

_____

_____

_____

_____

_____

_____

_____

_____

_____

_____

_____

_____

_____

_____

_____

_____

_____

_____

_____

Day 9

Focus! Focus! Focus!

A wise woman once told me, "If you keep looking in the rearview mirror, you're going to crash!" Although she was giving me a narrative of my life, this statement is true, literally. If you're driving and constantly looking in the rearview mirror, you will most likely crash into something or someone. Even if you keep your eyes straight and focus on what is in front of you, you still have limited ability to see what lies ahead. Imagine being stuck in traffic. You roll down the window to see what happened, but only to see countless cars in front of you.

How many times have you thought about your past and absolutely regretted it? Alternatively, how many times have you reminisced about your past and wished you were still there? ***Dwelling on the past, the good and bad, leaves you stuck.*** There is nothing you can do to change the past, and staying stuck in the past can hinder your future. So, what should you focus on? You don't know the future (God will reveal things to you in His time), so what do you do?

Focus on today.......

Often times people are so consumed with what they want to do in the future or crippled by what happened in their past they do not enjoy "the day." If you don't live in the present, in the now, then you're not living. ***Enjoy the days God gives you, and just be.*** Plan for the future, yes. Learn from your past mistakes, but most importantly, live and focus on the moment. ***Don't overwhelm yourself regarding the future. Don't limit yourself because of your past. God is always at work.***

MATTHEW 6:34

34 Therefore, do not worry about tomorrow, for tomorrow will worry about itself. Each day has enough trouble of its own.

yahweh

Yahweh (Jehovah, the great "I am") is one of the names for God. It means the self-existent One. He has always existed and will always exist. You can always rely on Him because He is your eternal source of strength.

References
(Genesis 2:4, Isaiah 40:3; 10; 1 Samuel 1:20; Exodus 6:1-4, 3:1-22)

Reflection

Don't dwell on the past. Don't worry about the future. What should you focus on today?

_____

_____

_____

_____

_____

_____

_____

_____

_____

_____

_____

_____

_____

_____

_____

_____

_____

_____

_____

_____

Day 10
Crazy In Love!

God knows the number of hairs on your head. *(Luke 12:7)*

His thoughts about you outnumber the grains of sand. *(Psalms 139:17-18)*

He died for you. *(Romans 5:8)*

You were created in His image. *(Genesis 1:27)*

He formed you. *(Jeremiah 1:5)*

He will never leave you nor forsake you. *(Deuteronomy 31:8)* You are always on His mind. *(Psalm 139:17:18)*

You belong to Him. *(Isaiah 43:1)*

He does ot want you to put anyone or anything before Him, He is a jealous God. *(Exodus 34:14)*

You are His daughter. *(1 John 3:1)*

He will fight for you. *(Psalms 11:7)*

Nothing can separate you from God's love. *(Romans 8:35-39)*

God's love for you is too great to fully comprehend. *(Ephesians 3:18-19)*

God can't help it! He loves you; He is love; no strings attached. *(1 John 4:8)*

You don't have to worry about Him leaving you, He is faithful now and forever. *(Deuteronomy 7:9)*

He wants you to be with Him forever. *(John 3:16)*

He loved you even when you did not know Him. *(Romans: 8)*

He loved you before you loved Him. *(1 John 4:19)*

God does NOT have anger issues. *(Psalm 86:15)*

You are the apple of His eye. *(Zechariah 2: 8)*

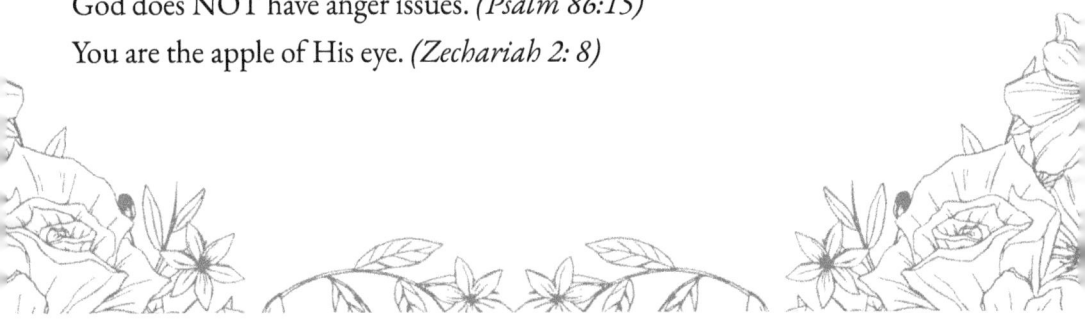

Love.

God is **LOVE.**

References
(1 Corinthians 13:4-8a, 1 John 4:8)

Reflection

_____

_____

_____

_____

_____

_____

_____

_____

_____

_____

_____

_____

_____

_____

_____

_____

_____

_____

_____

_____

_____

_____

_____

_____

Day 11

Don't Complain About The Weather!

It seems people are never satisfied. I wonder how God feels when we constantly complain about the weather. In the summer it's too hot, in the winter it's too cold. In the fall, the weather is unpredictable. Instead of complaining about the weather, embrace it. After all, it's out of your control. Complaining about the rain won't make it stop. Complaining about the hot sun won't make it disappear.

Just like the weather, life is unpredictable. Things are simply going to change. We are going to feel uncomfortable, inconvenienced, and disappointed. ***However, complaining should not be your default response.*** Just know that God makes all things work for our good, according to Romans 8:28. Not complaining and grumbling about something worth complaining about is not easy, but what good is complaining going to do?

So don't complain about the weather. We have absolutely no control over it. ***God is in control of everything.*** He holds everything in the palm of His hands.

PHILIPPIANS 2:14

14 Do everything without complaining and arguing...

El Shaddai

El Shaddai (Almighty God). El Shaddai is all powerful. Nothing is impossible for Him. El Shaddai is able to supply all your needs. He is all-sufficient. He has absolute power over all things and situations. God is able to fulfill all His promises and provide for His people in a powerful and loving way.

References
(Isaiah 41:10, Matthew 8:27, Exodus 6:2-3)

Reflection

We all have some valid reasons to complain and grumble. Find scripture to speak life over your situation instead of speaking death.

_____

_____

_____

_____

_____

_____

_____

_____

_____

_____

_____

_____

_____

_____

_____

_____

_____

_____

_____

_____

_____

_____

_____

Day 12
Beautifully Broken

To be beautifully broken means **to be placed in a season to be brought low, emptied, hurt, shaken, to suffer despair for one purpose.** You were beautifully broken so you could cry out to God and become fully His. No, this pain is not wasted! You may have been broken or still are, but you are NOT damaged. It's painful, yes, but **there is beauty on the other side of brokenness.**

ISAIAH 61:3

To grant those who mourn in Zion, Giving them a garland instead of ashes, The oil of gladness instead of mourning, The mantle of praise instead of a spirit of fainting. So they will be called oaks of righteousness, The planting of the LORD, that He may be glorified

Jehovah Shalom

Jehovah Shalom (The Lord is our peace). God brings peace to our troubled hearts and relieves us of our burdens.

References
(Isaiah 57:20, 21, Judges 6:23)

Reflection

Day 13
No Shame

Shame is the core root of low self-esteem, people-pleasing, comparison, self-hatred, jealousy, and the like. ***Being rooted in shame bears rotten fruit.*** To go a step further, being rooted in anything but Jesus bears rotten fruit. Shame, however, can be both detrimental and enlightening. A dear friend told me shame can be either a feeling or a belief.

For example, if you accidentally bump into someone at the store and don't apologize, you can start to feel shame because you did something to cause someone else pain to some extent. Alternatively, this feeling can be good because it convicts you of something you did wrong and, at the same time, makes you aware of it.

Shame can also be a belief, such as, "There is something wrong with me, she is so much better than me, I never do anything right, I am flawed, therefore I can't...."

So, what do you do with the shame that's consuming you?

Give it to God. Give it to those you trust. What I mean is confess your shame to God, verbally, expect him to set you free from this burden, because He will. You will see it fade away over time as He speaks to you and brings people into your life to help you navigate this healing journey. The people He puts in your life or the people you trust can take some shame away from you. Confess how you feel to someone. Let them hear what you have to say. ***If they love you and want to help you, their words can bring healing to your soul through the power of the Holy Spirit.*** A lot of the time, how you feel and what you believe about yourself is the complete opposite in someone's eyes.

Jehovah Tsidkenu

Jehovah Tsidkenu - God alone provides righteousness, ultimately in the person of His Son, Jesus Christ the Messiah, who became sin for us "that we might become the Righteousness of God in Him."

References
(Jeremiah 23:6, 2 Corinthians 5:21)

Reflection

Meditate on these scriptures today.

If we confess our sins, he is faithful and just and will forgive us our sins and purify us from all unrighteousness.

1 John 1:9

"There is, therefore, now no condemnation to those who are in Christ Jesus, who do not walk according to the flesh but according to the Spirit."

Romans 8:1

O Lord, in You, I have found a safe place. Let me never be ashamed. Set me free, because You do what is right and good.

Psalm 31:1

"As far as the east is from the west, so far has He removed our transgressions from us."

Psalm 103:12

_____

_____

_____

_____

_____

_____

_____

_____

_____

_____

Day 14
Yes, Master?

"People are slaves to whatever has mastered them."

2 Peter 2:19

This scripture is sobering and very profound! You can be mastered by fear, anxiety, depression, sex, drugs, procrastination, people pleasing, alcohol, him or her, your emotions, and all the above.

When we let God master our lives, anything and anyone not of God will leave... just watch!

What or who has mastered
(gained control of, overcome) you?
Be honest with God and yourself

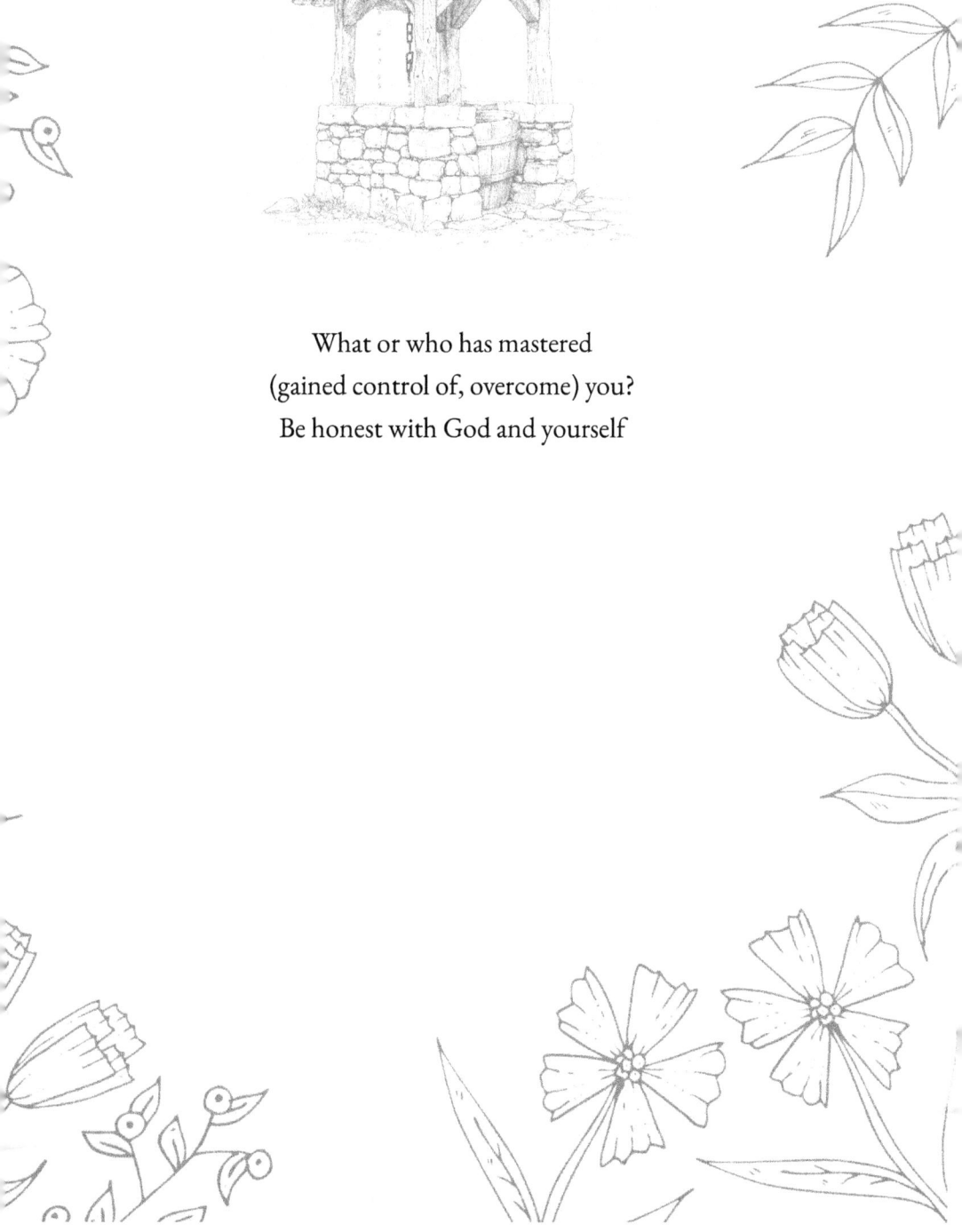

Adonai

Adonai means "master" or "Lord," showing God has sovereignty over us.

References
(1 Samuel 24:8, 2 Kings 2:19)

Reflection

Day 15
"It Is What It Is."

So, you are not where you want to be in life. Your kids are out of control, you are still single or unhappily married, you have gained ten pounds, and most days, your hair looks a mess. To top it off, your car is on its last leg!

You may not have experienced these circumstances in particular, but we all have dealt with our share of difficulties that seem to happen back-to-back.

Sometimes everything is going right, sometimes everything is going wrong, and oftentimes it's a little bit of both. I'm not saying to give up or stop caring, but sometimes we have to accept the fact that "it is what it is." Give what you can't control to God. ***Embrace the fact your life is not perfect, but you're still here.*** It's ok not to be ok. It's ok to not look your best every day or even feel your best. Life happens, but God makes everything work for our good (Romans 8:28), and God makes everything beautiful in its time (Ecclesiastes 3:11). Give God your issues; he is more than able to help you through them. Also, remember, that ***God does not "fix"everything. Sometimes, you have to go through it, but remember you have everything you need in Him.***

PHILIPPIANS 4:11-13

11 I am not saying this because I am in need, for I have learned to be content, whatever the circumstances. 12 I know what it is to be in need, and I know what it is to have plenty. I have learned the secret of being content in any and every situation, whether well-fed or hungry, whether living in plenty or in want. 13 I can do all this through him who gives me strength

Jehovah-Jireh

Jehovah-Jireh (The Lord will provide). This name embodies God's continual provision.

Reference
(Genesis 22:14)

Reflection

Epilogue
So why choose Jesus?

I know you may be thinking, *"I pray all the time, but it's not helping my situation," or "Where is God?"* I can only tell you from experience that choosing Jesus is the only way to peace in your life. True peace. Not the superficial "peace" when you go on vacation or have the house to yourself. What I mean by choosing Jesus is choosing to simply pray and believe. *Pray, believe, and wait.* He is real, as real as your therapist, your friends, or anyone you rely heavily on for comfort.

Is this journey easy? Absolutely not! You will go through periods of loneliness, and He may even isolate you from people. It's ok! It will not be this way forever. Let God have you to Himself and just love on you. Try your best to humbly accept His love and provision.

I say all this because I truly and deeply want women to be healed so we can do the things God has called us to do and fulfill our purpose. Whatever plans you had for your life may even change when you encounter Jesus, sis. That's ok too! He loves you so much to see you go through life with pain and turmoil in your soul. I know this firsthand. Let God love you and lead you out of the darkness.

Meet the Author

Joy Mullins

Meet the Author

In this series of devotionals, Joycelyn "Joy" offers insights and experiences to empower and support women in maintaining their faith in God during challenging times. Her devotionals provide a source of encouragement for women facing life challenges.

As a mother of four boys and resident of Atlanta, Georgia, her personal experiences and growing relationship with God have woven into the fabric of her writing journey. She is committed to fostering open conversations around women, mental health, and faith. Her prayer is that her devotionals will encourage and empower women dealing with struggles from all walks of life. She aims to provide a compassionate perspective rooted in faith through the lens of Christ-centered devotionals.

To contact the Author:

Follow on Instagram @wildflower080602
Website: wildflowerdevo.com
Facebook: Wildflower Devotionals (J Nakia Mullins)
Email: wildflowerdevotionals@gmail.com

Milton Keynes UK
Ingram Content Group UK Ltd.
UKHW030740121124
451094UK00011B/707